THE COMPLETE CLARINET PLAYER
BOOK 2
by Paul Harvey.

'By the end of this book, you
will know more about music and you
will be playing thirty-four popular
songs including *Sunny, Ain't She Sweet,
Fiddler On The Roof* and *Lucille.*'

Paul Harvey

EXCLUSIVELY DISTRIBUTED BY

HAL•LEONARD®

This book © Copyright 1986, 1994 by Wise Publications
Order No. AM62621
ISBN 0-7119-0878-8

Art direction by Mike Bell.
Designed by Sands Straker Studios Limited.
Diagrams by Mark Straker.
Photography by Peter Wood.
Arranged by Paul Harvey.
Clarinet supplied by Bill Lewington Limited.

Your Guarantee of Quality
As publishers, we strive to produce every
book to the highest commercial standards.
Throughout, the printing and binding of this book have
been planned to ensure a sturdy, attractive publication
which should give years of enjoyment.
If your copy fails to meet our high standards,
please inform us and we will gladly replace it.

CONTENTS

About This Book

When you finished Book 1 you had learnt the bottom register fingerings in the keys of F and G.
Book 2 starts by filling in all the gaps in the bottom register so that you can play any song, however chromatic, in the range from bottom E up to middle B♭.

Then it is time to move up to the upper register and learn the principle of how the register key makes the bottom register go up a twelfth.

The most difficult thing to learn on the clarinet is joining these two registers (crossing the break) and the whole of Book 3 will be devoted to this.

But this step will be made much easier if you first have a solid grounding in both registers separately, and a firm understanding of the fingering comparisons between the bottom and upper registers.

For this reason, Book 2 of The Complete Clarinet Player finishes with a section which is unique to this Tutor. Sixteen well known songs have been especially selected and arranged so that they can be played entirely in the upper register range:

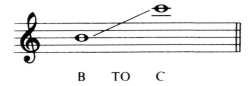

B   TO   C

Each is written first in the bottom register, then with the *same fingering* in the upper register, just by adding the register key.

This system of practice is invaluable for laying a sound foundation for crossing the break at the next stage.

Session 1:
THE REST OF THE NOTES IN THE BOTTOM REGISTER

There are only four more notes to learn in the bottom register. The first is:

C sharp which can also be called D flat

Every *Sharp,* called by the letter of the note *Below* it, can also be called the *Flat* of the note *Above* it. So, the B♭'s we learnt in Book 1 can also be called A sharp, and the F sharps can be called G♭.

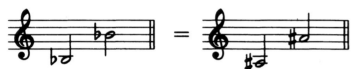

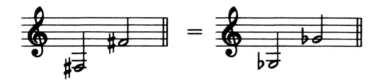

C sharp is fingered with *all* your left hand: like C, plus your left little finger on the nearest key.

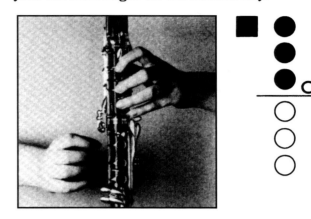

E flat (D sharp) is fingered with your left hand, playing D, and your right finger No. 1 opening the nearest side key.

Bottom G sharp (A flat) is fingered like bottom G, plus your right little finger opening the nearest key on the top row.

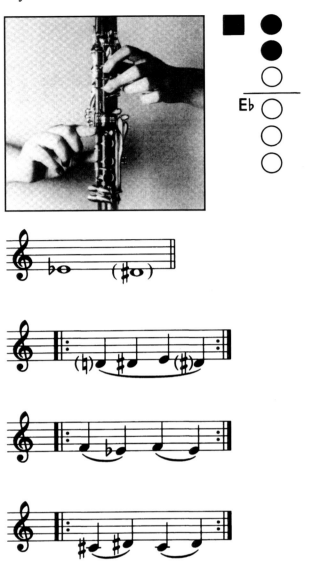

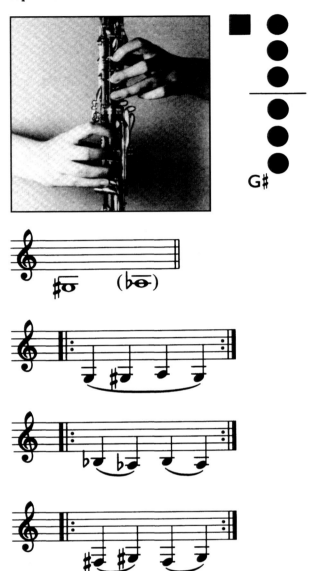

Middle G sharp (A flat) is fingered by your left first finger opening the key next to the A key.

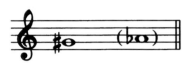

This note is an octave above bottom G sharp (A♭)

OB-LA-DI, OB-LA-DA *In the key of B♭*

Words & Music: John Lennon and Paul McCartney

The chord of B♭

In the key of A

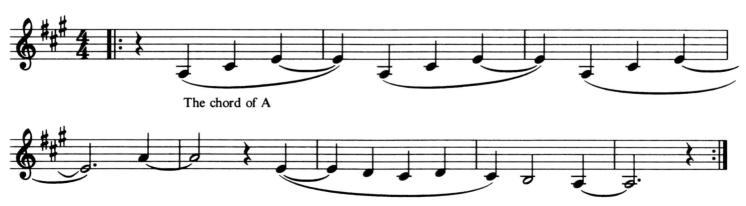

The chord of A

CHANSON D'AMOUR

Words & Music: Wayne Shanklin

These three versions of the song "Show Me The Way
To Go Home" provide very good practice for all our
new notes.

SHOW ME THE WAY TO GO HOME *In the key of B♭ (B♭'s and E♭'s)*

Words & Music: Irving King

In the key of F (B♭'s)

and an octave higher:

THE ETON BOATING SONG
Words & Music: Drummond & Wodehouse

In the key of A (F sharp, C sharp and G sharp)

Session 2: THE CHROMATIC SCALE

This is the most important thing to practise on any instrument, because it teaches you *all* the notes. It both ascends and descends in semitones (half steps) and is usually written in sharps going up:

and in flats going down

but don't forget, they are exactly the *same notes* up and down. The bottom three notes can be played in two different ways: first with the fingering you have already learnt:

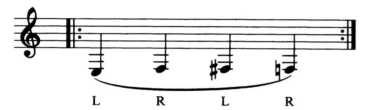

Keep your right little finger on the F key all the time: this is very important

Or, using these alternative fingerings:

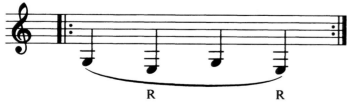

The main use of left F is before Ab, because Ab (G sharp) can only be played with your right little finger.

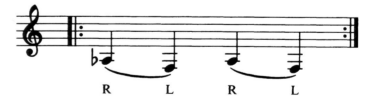

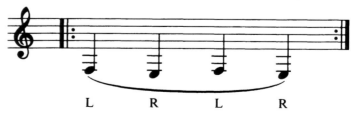

Keep your left little finger on the left F key.

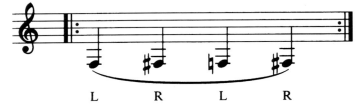

Keep your left little finger on the left F key.

Now practise

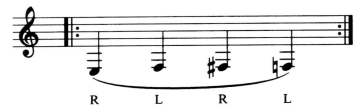

keeping your left little finger on the left F key all the time.

Now practise the chromatic scale in four note groups like this:

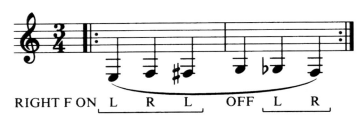

RIGHT F ON L R L   OFF L R

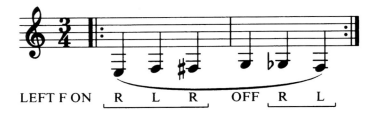

LEFT F ON R L R   OFF R L

(Don't forget, F sharp = G flat).

Now move up to the next group:

(G♯ = A♭)

In the next group there is one very important new alternative fingering; chromatic B natural, fingered like B♭, plus right finger No. *3* (*not* no. 2) on the chromatic B key.

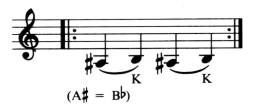

(A♯ = B♭)

Now practise the four note group:

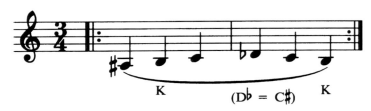

K   (D♭ = C♯)   K

All the other groups are played with fingerings you already know.

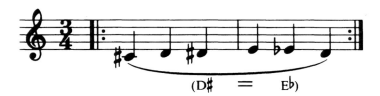

(D♯ = E♭)

(F♯ = G♭)

(G♯ = A♭)

Always use a chromatic scale over whatever range you have learnt, as a warm up exercise, because it checks that all the keys are working properly and that none of the pads are sticking to the holes. Now you are ready to play songs which contain bits of the chromatic scale.

CRUISING DOWN THE RIVER

Words & Music: Eily Beadell and Nell Tollerton

IF I HAD YOU *In the key of F:*

Words & Music: Ted Shapiro, Jimmy Campbell and Reg Connelly

Why not try the bottom chromatic group in the two
different ways. Don't forget to keep your F key down
for the first three notes, whichever side you're on.

In the key of C:

Session 3: STARTING THE UPPER REGISTER

Play a C with all your left hand on:

While you are blowing the C, open the *Register Key* on the back of the clarinet with your left thumb.
But be sure that your thumb is still covering the hole as well; it is necessary for it to touch only the very tip of the register key.

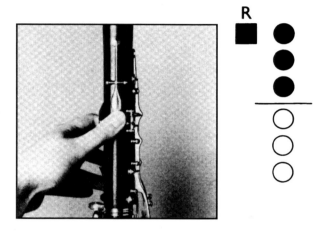

This is what will happen if you do it correctly:

The C has gone up *Twelve* notes, to G in the upper register.

Now do the same thing on B♭, and it will go up to F:

A goes up to E:

G goes up to D:

and F goes up to C:

Play this in the bottom register:

Add the register key and it becomes:

C D E F G F E D

15

Play this song in the bottom register first:

I KNOW WHERE I'M GOIN'

Words & Music: Herbert Hughes

Now open the register key with your left thumb, (mind you keep the thumb hole covered as well), use the same right hand fingerings as in the bottom register, and you will play your first song in the upper register.

BANKS OF THE OHIO *In the bottom register:*

Traditional

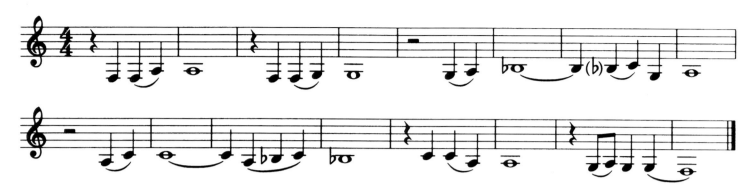

Add the register key:

Refer back to session 9 in Book 1 for the bottom register
fingering of "This Ole House". Add the register key,
and hear it go up a twelfth.

THIS OLE HOUSE

Words & Music: Stuart Hamblen

Session 4: EXTENDING THE UPPER REGISTER

The lowest note of the upper register is B; E goes up to B:

D goes up to A:

Keep the C key down.

Play this in the bottom register:

Add the register key and it becomes:

C   B   C   D   E   F   G   A   G   F   E   D

GOD SAVE THE QUEEN *in the key of C*

Traditional   (Refer to session 10 in Book 1 for bottom register fingering in F, then add register key).

Here are some more songs you played in the bottom
register in Session 9 in Book 1.
Just add the register key, and *up* they go!

MICHAEL ROW THE BOAT ASHORE
Traditional

WHEN THE SAINTS GO MARCHING IN
Traditional

Session 5:
GETTING TO THE TOP OF THE UPPER REGISTER

E goes up to B:

play

and F goes up to C

Add the register key:

G   A   B   C

C is the highest note in the upper register.

Add the register key:

C   B   C   D   E   F   G   A   B   C   B   A   G   F   E   D

BARBARA ALLEN
Traditional

DRINK TO ME ONLY WITH THINE EYES

Traditional

THE FIRST NOWELL

Traditional

SUNNY
Words & Music: Bobby Hebb

WINCHESTER CATHEDRAL
Words & Music: Geoff Stephens

Session 6:
FILLING IN THE REST OF THE UPPER REGISTER NOTES

F sharp (G♭) goes up to C sharp (D♭):

A♭ (G sharp) goes up to E♭ (D sharp):

B natural goes up to F sharp (G♭):

C sharp (D♭) goes up to G sharp (A♭):

and E♭ (D sharp) goes up to B♭ (A sharp):

Now you can practise the chromatic groups from session 2; same fingering as the bottom register, plus the register key.

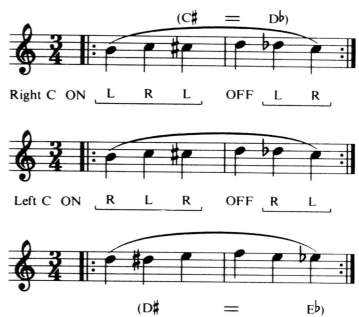

Right C ON   L   R   L   OFF   L   R

Left C ON   R   L   R   OFF   R   L

(D♯   =   E♭)

Use the chromatic key for F sharp, (Right finger no. 3) just like chromatic B natural in the bottom register.

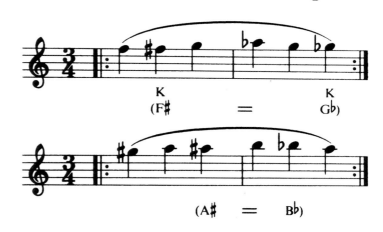

K   K
(F♯   =   G♭)

(A♯   =   B♭)

And one more group to bring us to the top of the upper register:

BYE BYE LOVE
Words & Music: Felice & Boudleaux Bryant

PAPERBACK WRITER
Words & Music: John Lennon and Paul McCartney

Session 7:
MORE SONGS TO COMPARE THE REGISTERS

The rest of this book is devoted to songs containing all the fingerings learnt in the bottom register, then each song is repeated with the *same fingering*, but the addition of the register key taking it up a twelfth into the upper register.

This gives a solid foundation from which to proceed to Book 3, which is entirely concerned with crossing the break. It strengthens the sound in the upper register, and teaches the different notes obtainable with the same fingerings from one register to the other.

THREE LITTLE FISHES

Words & Music: Saxie Dowell

Add register key

The sign **C** stands for *Common Time*, which is just another name for 4/4 time.

When the **C** has a line through it, **¢** it is called Alla Breve, or Cut Common Time and means that the music has a two in a bar feel, rather than four in a bar, although mathematically it is still exactly the same as 4/4 time.

AIN'T SHE SWEET

Words: Jack Yellen   Music: Milton Ager

Add register key

ON THE CREST OF A WAVE

Words & Music: Ralph Reader

Add register key

This song uses an alternative fingering, called Long E♭ in the bottom register, and Long B♭ in the upper register. The fingering is E/B natural with the left hand, plus first finger right hand.

This fingering is used when E♭/B♭ follows B♭/F or any note below it. Never use Long E♭/B♭ in scale passages, however; they are always the normal side key fingering.

TULIPS FROM AMSTERDAM

English Words: Gene Martyn   Original Words: Neumann and Bader   Music: Ralf Arnie

Add register key

LITTLE GIRL

Words & Music: Madeline Hyde & Francis Henry

Add register key

A GARDEN IN THE RAIN

Words: James Dyrenforth   Music: Carroll Gibbons

Add register key

FIDDLER ON THE ROOF

Music: Jerry Bock   Lyrics: Sheldon Harnick

Add register key

THE MARINES' HYMN

Words & Music: L. Z. Phillips

Add register key

LUCILLE

Words & Music: Roger Bowling and Hal Bynum

Add register key

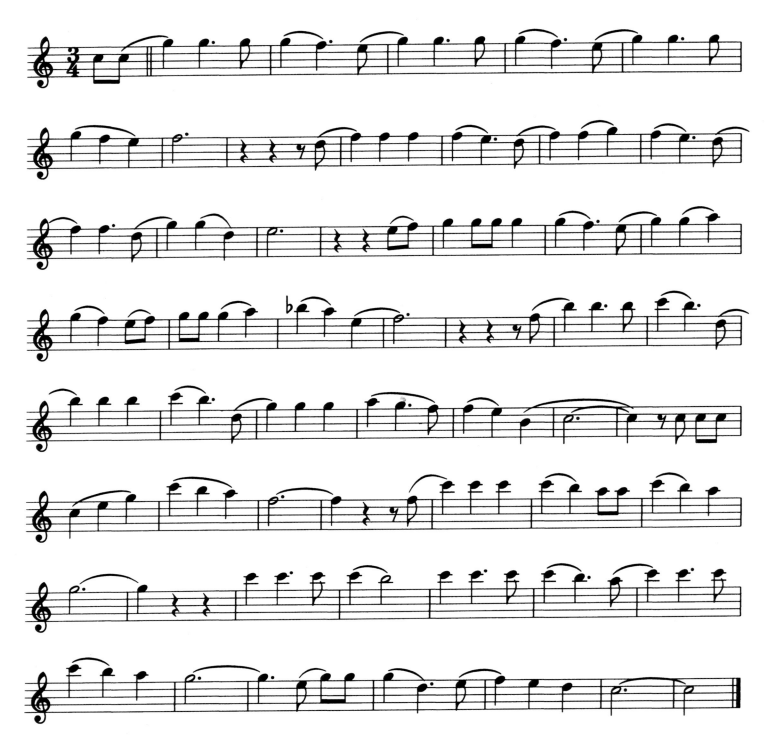

I'M IN A DANCING MOOD

Words & Music: Maurice Sigler, Al Goodhart and Al Hoffman

Add register key

EVERYDAY

Words & Music: Charles Hardin and Norman Petty

Add register key

CAROLINA MOON

Words: Benny Davis   Music: Joe Burke

Long E♭

Add register key

Long B♭

Session 8:
SONGS COMPARING THE REGISTERS IN HARDER KEYS

Although the fingerings may at first appear to be harder in these keys, bear in mind that they are, in fact, easier to play, staying in one register or the other, than a song in an easier looking key which crosses between the registers. That is what we shall be learning to do in Book 3.

DRIFTING AND DREAMING Key of A: F sharp, C sharp and G sharp.
Words: Haven Gillespie   Music: Egbert Van Alstyne, Erwin R. Schmidt and Loyal Curtis

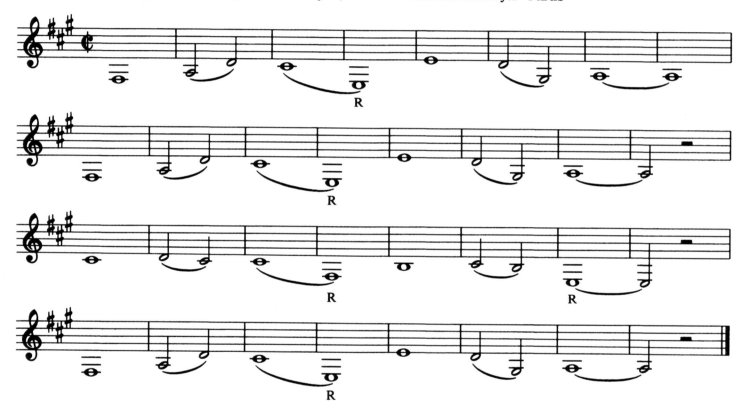

Add register key

Key of E: D sharp as well.

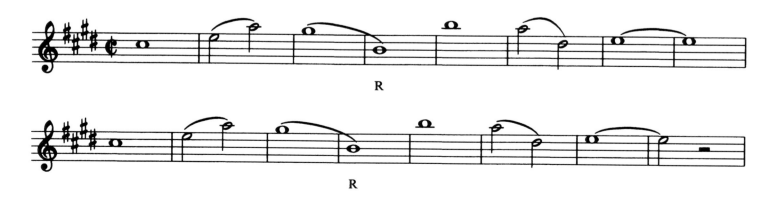

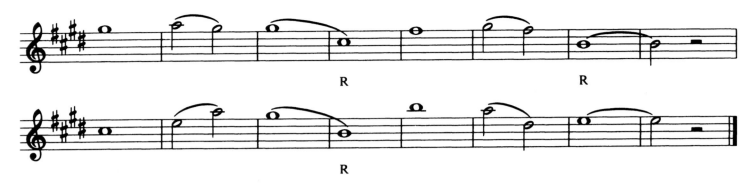

THE LONESOME ROAD

Words: Gene Austin   Music: Nathaniel Shilkret

I CAN'T GIVE YOU ANYTHING BUT LOVE

Key of A♭: B♭'s, E♭'s, A♭'s and D♭'s.

Words: Dorothy Fields Music: Jimmy McHugh

Long E♭

Add register key

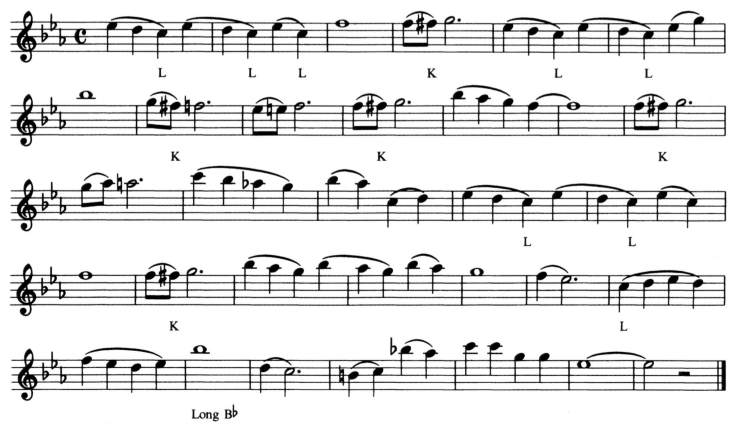

Long B♭

GIRL OF MY DREAMS
Key of Db: Bb's, Eb's, Ab's, Db's, and Gb's.

Words & Music: Sunny Clapp

Add register key

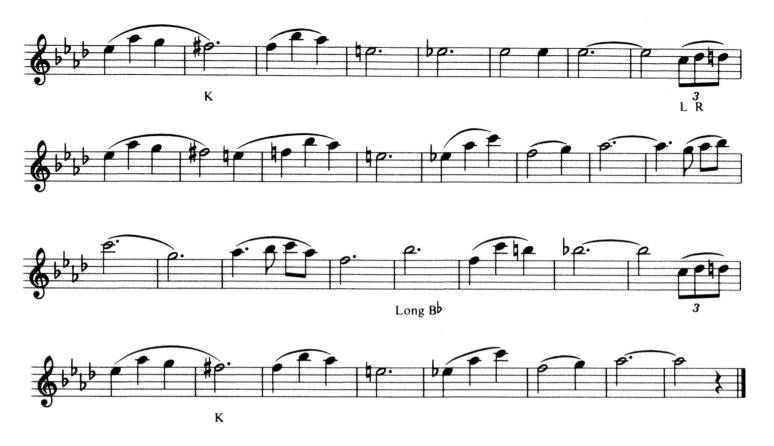

K

L R 3

Long B♭

3

K

THE REST OF THE BOTTOM REGISTER
SCALES AND CHORDS

B♭ MAJOR

A MAJOR

A♭ MAJOR

E MAJOR

F# MAJOR

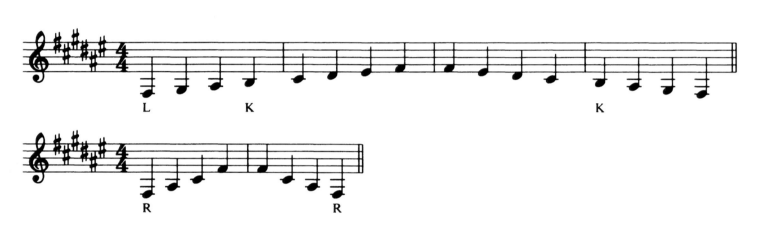

In Book Three you will learn how to join the lower and upper registers of the clarinet, commonly called 'crossing the break'. Popular songs including Yesterday, Money, Money, Money Climb Every Mountain and Spanish Eyes have been specially arranged to illustrate this important step in your progress. Examples of playing songs in the upper register are given, together with tips on constructive practice techniques.